Also by Thomas A Clark
from Carcanet Press

—

*Yellow & Blue*
2014

*The Hundred Thousand Places*
2009

# Farm by the Shore

THOMAS A CLARK

CARCANET

First published in Great Britain in 2017 by
CARCANET PRESS LTD
Alliance House, 30 Cross Street
Manchester M2 7AQ
www.carcanet.co.uk

A CIP catalogue record for this book is available
from the British Library: ISBN 9781784103521.

Design: Luke Allan.
Printed and bound in England by SRP Ltd.

The publisher acknowledges financial assistance
from Arts Council England.

FARM BY THE SHORE

sea separates from sky
earth from sea
all things take shape
from darkness

do you know the land
where bog cotton grows

on the littoral
among the laminarias
at the equinoctial
low spring tide
the tonality or ethos
of a floating world
is pooled in rock
in wrack and tangle

nothing is lovelier
than the grey line
that approaches and departs
from precision


in the truce of the morning
the bitter taste
of the memory of talk
a debris in the wake
of eagerness

green floats in the mist and haze
then green floats in the haze
then green floats

for the nurture
of all things is moist
warmth itself coming
to be from the moist
the seeds of all things
being moist in nature

an island balanced on a line of light
a ship sailing through the sky




a blue bird
that makes its nest
on a calm sea
and in the woven
water lays
three blue eggs

before the coming of snow
long strings of deer
make their way down the hillside
the straths fill with them
as the mind is full
at the thought of them
before the coming of snow


don't flinch away
let the wind slice through
defensive attitudes
connective tissue
ramparts of the hill fort

high snow slopes
sweetened by wind
touch blue
to draw the eye
to cornices
brushstrokes




glittering in gneiss
snowflakes on eyelashes
frail songs by torrents

in reduced visibility
going is staying
in the little territory




it would seem
to be the sum
of perceptions
for what is not
perceived is not

each time sing a long tone
into the drone of the wind
then adjust it up or down
closer to the drone of the wind




between stimulus and response
the grey lag

stratus cumulus nimbus
where you look you go
cirrus altostratus


perceptions are dew
people are mist
days are thistledown


everything melts
but the snow is sheltered
for a while by a wall

as yet some part
of your mind
is limestone
skeletons of coral
petrified crinoid
feeling welling up

so dark in the well
so clear in the light
so sweet on the lips
so cold in the throat

it takes all the mass
and momentum
of a mountain
to intimidate its own
contingency




if it comes towards you
at the exact speed
as you go towards it
in expectation
get out of the way

climbing up onto
the mountain's shoulder
you step above yourself
to be among mountains
that stand around in the cold




a stone from the shore
carried in the rucksack
to act as a ballast
to the impetus of summits

on a clear day
while the mountains
turn in a dance
to a reel
or slip jig
join in the mad
mountain dance


by the rush of a torrent
in the din of the flow
listen to tighten
the strings of the harp

but come consider
how each thing is
presented to trust
to sight or taste
to thought or touch

for there are these alone
pouring through one another
dallying with one another
intermingling
the hot the cold the wet the dry
in motion change and time
coming together and parting
for shapes never tire of shifting

yellow shines through the mist and haze
then yellow shines through the haze
then yellow shines




here are waterfalls
that flow upward
hills that dip
their heads in pools
roads that idle
in sorrel

if you have to sail
through a storm to reach it
or trek into it
knee-deep through a bog
it's not nature
if you need to inspect it
through a microscope
on a cold day
hanging from a cliff


a summer walker
you climbed no higher
than the lower slopes
delayed by blaeberries
and lack of ambition

the trust of the first
celandines opening
the first of the trust

between gorse and coltsfoot
the yellowhammer
between coltsfoot and gorse

anyone who comes
to yellow wants
more

a prodigality of skylarks
a liberality of skylarks
a virtuosity of skylarks
a spontaneity of skylarks


you could be
extravagantly
straightforward
you might be
categorically
at ease

crocuses crowding
thick on the bank
in clusters under trees
build to a chorus
as the colour fills

a long tendril
to twist and twine
a tender intuition
at the end of the stem
allows the tufted vetch
to cling and climb
to clamber
over the hedge

quicker than tadpoles
in pools the shadows
of tadpoles in pools
or the notion of shadows
of tadpoles in pools




the wren has entered
an exacting freedom
within the thicket
of prepositions

the stone
in your hand
is a shape
in your hand
the weight
in your hand
is cold


do you feel you must reach
for a separate name
distinct from the grain
beneath your fingers

deposits of sediments
longshore drift
plate tectonics
sleep in the afternoon




born from thunder
damsel fly

the force or inertia
that brought the boulder
to lodge against the birch
is irreducible


a man bending over a pool
reaching in to take
something from the pool
takes something
from the pool


many a good man
sings to himself

much that is light
outshines itself
dazed in a grace
that comes to it
as unimpeded movement
it throws a thought
and catches it
farther on


not as a stranger
you move surely
through the lonely places
surely not a stranger

familiar of the salt marsh
of the dune slack the machair
familiar with the pasture
the set aside

sitting on a rock
having kinship with rock
of one impulse with
waves and wheat

ubiquitous frog noise
loud and harsh joy
of raw altered states
drone with flute and harmonium
scraped singing bowls

distance and proximity
a downhill tumble
proximity and distance
through the downy willow
distance and proximity

there are practices
to augment experience
over-ruling lore
habits that allow
for exception
dispositions that bring
faculties to vision

the term undoes its negation
you pine for what you deny
the shade is deep and fragrant
in a forest without trees

noun intending its object
stoat chasing a rabbit

the weavers of tales
and the spinners of fates
are in collusion

a splash of cold
water on the wrists
you survive
your absences



a thin trickle
of water through
the watercress
is enough

small brown bird throat white
breast suffused with peach
hidden in a glancing light
vanishes when it stops singing


a warbler among the leaves
as if the leaves
had come to the notion
of a warbler among the leaves

by the side of a road
relentless in heat and dust
sycamores store darkness
great reserves of coolness


under the branches
everything dissolves
in coolness
a stillness
spreads through anything
that moves

light builds a darkness
within the tree
to a shock of cold
or transparency




no practice
for shade
but a practice
of shade




they found the shapes in trees
to build the boats to follow
sea lanes to spices

in the graphite shade
the cracked black pepper
grain of the wood
everything drifts




through the long grass
something runs
from predication and assumption
into possibility
almost successfully

complexity is distributed
across the birch scrub
at a glance a movement
is described and redescribed
swiftly across the birch scrub

although the branches are still
they reach out across
the space to other branches
you will see or feel
their branching as reaching
although the branches are still

a turbulence in water
a perturbation of the air
thrills through the wood as cold
or a water song in leaves




a trembling
in the leaves
gathers beyond
its impetus
a commotion
or contagion
in the leaves

as you move through the trees
they shift around you
jostling for position
until everything you see
has sight of you




something only
glimpsed is something
something barely
discerned is something
something hardly
there is something

deer and shade
trunk and torso
nominal distinctions




antlers locked with sunbeams
peeled velvet
moss

things are vibrations
that steady
briefly
their locality
is variable
a continual tending
or tuning
to the place




second
person
singular
or plural

of bodies changed to new shapes
of minds changed
the breeze informs you
the shadows tell you
of garments into foliage
limbs to branches




through the gesture
the impulse
in the gesture
flows
carried to
a liberty
only the gesture
allows

variation is the way of heaven
try on this shape
try on that shape
in mimicry of integrity
approach it


try on this colour
try on that colour
how do they suit
your complexion


dark blue light blue
winter green hunter green
olive mahogany tan
deep mauve dark plum

under the chords and clavichords
of the river in the wood
all the sympathetic
strings sound


wayward impulse
owned by no one
blown moth


a breeze that stirred
a word you heard
shifting the balance

glades in woods unvisited
unvisited glades in woods
glades in words unvisited




how did you get here
your mind wandering
what grace guided your steps




green one of the wood

a place to which
you might retreat
retire or repair
to petition for nuance
perhaps to drop
to sleep a bit
to learned distinctions
a wish for shade
granted




grapes of the north
raindrops

colour is balance
a shade or a tone
something in between
mint and thyme


ovals of light
are sprinkled over
scattered chickweed
wintergreen


here muntjac deer
browse oxlip flowers
leaving the leaves
unbruised

gean and juniper
the small-leaved lime
rowan and alder
take your time


fluttering dove
dove hovering
settling dove


written in shadow
a short history
of delay

propriety might stretch
a dandelion rope
across the trees
giving pause




how it worries
away at conviction
the flicker of everything
at the edge of attention

hart's tongue and adder's spit
fern fronds unfurling
croziers of bladder fern
volutes of bracken
spleenwort and polypody


light beside bracken
light on bracken
light behind bracken


a comma resting
on the path,

on bright days when the wood
is veiled in blue light
light in the wood seems
to be a light of the wood
given out while contained




perhaps the more
need not appear
if it is there
in support
or suggestion
there is more

alder and oak and birch
hawthorn rowan willow
talk to each other again
lime and larch and pine
whitebeam gean hazel

the wound
of the sound
of an axe
in the wood
aches

sons and daughters of early risers
would steal the light from your door
daughters and sons of early risers
on a fine day ask for more




the slopes eroded
the land claimed
the rivers braided
the burns dammed

a volume of coarse-grained sediment
is hurried along a gradient
in a specific gravity of water
until erosion is deposited
in islands and bars separated
by multiple channels or braids
zones of confluence and diffluence


the immediate heirs
of the present holder
each have equal
entitlement to land
everyone gets a share
of wind and rain
of arable and bog
even to ruinous
fragmentation

who knocks
at the door
who stands
on the threshold
who blocks
the light
from the porch


rumour slander innuendo
stick to the names
of far-flung clans
status is a stake
in qualities
transported along rivers
into glens

a plant a herbivore a predator
and a predator of the predator
a space of distribution
and a time of predation


help with the peats
will be given in return for
help with the peats
support is in kind
but reciprocity
has its boundary
sheep may stray

it is better to be battered
by a second cousin
than beaten up
by a neighbour
consanguinity takes precedence
over contiguity
you would rather be throttled
by your mother's brother
than strangled
by a stranger


if you can hide
and not get caught
then run out
and kick the can
you are it

the dry ones
the long thin ones
who leaned in doorways long ago
who rolled their cigarettes in rain
they mould your cheekbones
they fur your arteries




in among the whins
there is a stone
once you could have read
the name on it

go able men
arrayed in most
warlike manner
running in foray
taking kye
oxen horses
gold and money
burning houses
mutilating many
to drink of gentle
blood and free
then ladies woe
shall cry

winds are disconsolate
burns flow circumspectly
birds mourn on the branches
since you have gone

the shapes and colours
have lost their relation
the surfaces miss
your hand on them

not for peace in the gloaming
not for space in the morning
not for silver or gold
will you return

the weaving and unravelling
of fragrant meadow grasses
the braiding and undoing
of hair-moss and willow
the tightening and loosening
of bonds of affection
the stretching and breaking
of long melodic strands
the spinning and extending
of strings of narrative
the twining and twisting
of dogwood and rowan


practice or pattern
according to reason
carried in tradition

a wad of wool
or flax is hooked
to the top of the distaff
then drawn out
towards the spindle
which is spun under
its own momentum
as the earth turns
round the sun


for a smooth yarn
wet the fibre
with your finger
as you spin

fishers for pearls
pine cone gatherers
shy folk
washed from the river bank
faded from the wood


land poor in itself
grazed and burnt
beaten by lashing rain
could regenerate again
to heathland and mire
herb rich grassland
scrub in mosaic


herons by pools
goldfinches at the seed heads
raptors over hills

here is what there is
the sure and present
sense of what there is

thick blanket bog peat

in and on the water on and in


a raft of sphagnum and sedges


anchored in mud or floating free


a buzzard circling under pondweed

the waters of the lochan
fanned by a breeze
run for the cover
of reeds and sedges
rocking the pondweed




as a sylph into silken waters
slip between the clean sheets
of the scent of mown hay

as I me went
by water side
full fast in mind
ran water sound
a lady bright
there gave me leave
to lay down lightly
by her


water that flows
through watercress
receives the qualities
of watercress

lapping of the little
waves at quiet
continual lapping
of the little waves
unquiet on quiet
the first harmonics

in the bud
there is the poise
of possibility
as if pausing
to anticipate
the waterlily

by the lap lapping of the water
the dip dipping of a dipper
in the light dapples over
over water and dipper


clouds among waterlilies
part leaving waterlilies
doubled in reflection
until the clarity clouds


gold leaf laid on water

moonwort milkwort
slender st john's wort
that they might be known
have their time in the sun
lousewort and bitter vetch


anyone who is given
a promise of happiness
should insist that it is
redeemed


ephemera…
food of swallows

what remains is pollen
pine stumps and spores
coleopteran fragments
evidence of clearance
of erosion or acidification
precariously preserved
in archives in bogs



meadows of windloving flowers
ferns and fungi and mosses
produce great quantities
of light-weight grains
of pollen to be distributed
broadly on currents of air

suspended in clouds
fossilised in rocks
hidden in the lint
in a jacket pocket
in furrows and fissures
dirt tracks and ditches


in pool and in hollow
deposits of the pollen
of sycamore and willow
deposits of the pollen
of meadowsweet and mallow
in pool and in hollow

when a warbler lights
on a tall grass
grass and warbler
dip
and right themselves
and swing


the things that mean most
are spoken of least


from
bog
myrtle

when the mare canters
across the meadow
a breeze stirs
the fragrant grasses


softly step
over the boundaries
in sunshine
without fear


brighter than soldiers
in all their armour
is the one you love
coming through clover

wetland and hazel woodland
species-rich grassland
tall herb communities
peat bog and coastal heath




keep the cattle out
let the meadow germinate
flower and seed
then let the cattle in




cut the silage late
after the seed has set
graze tightly in winter
to clean up the pasture

sheep and cattle on the hill
mountain hare in the margins
voles on the in-bye
transparent burnet moth


grass of parnassus
wood bitter vetch
scarce bog orchid
sword-leaved helleborine


lenticular cloud above the headland
a glee-club of goldfinches
the sea blue behind
devil's bit scabious

small oats rye bere barley
ripe harvest in late summer
a shallow ploughing
grazing and fallow in rotation


corncrake and corn bunting
great yellow bumble bee
oystercatcher lapwing golden plover
orchid vetch and clover


when no one is home
the strawberry roan
stands in the rain
forlorn

mattress of heather
of bracken or eelgrass
pillow of cottongrass
stuffed with a down
of coltsfoot or reedmace
floor strewn with bog myrtle




strong rope of heather
honeysuckle bridle
twisted birch bark tether
fish trap of sedge
purple moor-grass anchor rope

scatter rue across the floor
place rue among the linen
blue-leaved bitter-leaved rue
that springs anew
after burial in snow
set a bank of rue
herb of grace
restorer of vision
for there is much to see


open the door and startle a deer

of no particular gifts
having no particular intention
but to while or whittle the time
in ling and tormentil


good for nothing
but for taking
the idle road
to nothing but


the horse in the field is a horse
the word horse is a word
they are both a little hoarse

plenitude of the sensible
going down to the sea
as to a value as sure
as a sense of direction

an appetite for blue
precedes and survives
a quantity of blue
or qualities of grey
of gold or silver

in fidelity to clarity
the wounds in the rocks
open



blue sits beside green
green beside yellow
separately
each is its own
but shines in company

if you tell yourself to look
then to look more intently
you add imperative
to imperative
if you tell yourself to look
then to look less intently

warm light pours out
through the open door
but the door is too low
to give access

the well of virtues
how is it far


shells and pebbles
rags of linen
stuffs worn out
offered in tribute
pins and needles
rusty nails


the grove of delight
you are almost
there

go down to the boat
come to it
through the wet grass
against the slight
weight
of the wet grass


three knots in a rope
if you run into a storm
untie the first knot
if you run into a storm
untie the second knot
never untie the third knot

bird with a call
like a comb scraped
against a credit card
on tip toe go
through the hay ho
who will know



success is in excess
of the aspiration
it is a disappointment
sad horses stand
in gathering dusk
beside the ploughed field

smoke and wool snagged on wire
old stories told through smoke
smoke from burning carried away
scent of crushed rosemary and smoke
smoke screen of old stories
a theft of honey in a puff of smoke

wrap your blanket
of mist and cloud
woven of waiting
around me
my love

the grasses are flowering
the bracken is turning
the swallows are gathering


when you see the direction
of the melody
your fingers will follow
across the strings


fine lines of fracture
mended with gold

the cattle take
the same road
at the same time
every day
turn in
at the same gate
towards evening


as light fades from the hills
feeling pervades the fields
they are not at rest
while the light lasts

a mountain in mist and rain
you went there and returned
you are not the same


around sprigs of lavender
along the stems of sea holly
it is already evening


a child might take you
by the hand and lead you
to dusk at the wood's edge

sitting in the dusk
duration becomes substance
you could lay your hand on it




who knows where
the light ends
or the resonance
of the bell stops




the black stone from the shore
here it is on the black table

magick moonwort or honesty
dried peeled oval seedpods
little transparent hanging moons
or satin silver dollars
may be used to gather moonlit dew



the sound of the sea in your head
in the bed by the window
in the moonlight on the tide
on the pillow of a wave

your name is not heard
in the reeds by the lochan
where once the rocks
threw it back


a small fragment
of a golden sickle
dug out of moss